The Peter Paradox

The Peter Paradox

✦

Maturing through Mistakes

Dr. Larry W. Ellis

iUniverse, Inc.
New York Lincoln Shanghai

The Peter Paradox
Maturing through Mistakes

Copyright © 2006 by Larry W. Ellis

iUniverse books may be ordered through booksellers or by contacting:

iUniverse
2021 Pine Lake Road, Suite 100
Lincoln, NE 68512
www.iuniverse.com
1-800-Authors (1-800-288-4677)

ISBN-13: 978-0-595-36777-1 (pbk)
ISBN-13: 978-0-595-81195-3 (ebk)
ISBN-10: 0-595-36777-1 (pbk)
ISBN-10: 0-595-81195-7 (ebk)

Printed in the United States of America

My mother
Ora Mai Reese (in glory)
My wife
Vanderler L. Ellis
My children
Phillip (son-in-law), Tawana Shumpert
Justin
Austin

Contents

Acknowledgments

The staff, leadership team, and members of Pilgrim Baptist Church
San Mateo, California
Tynetta Brooks—Editor
Debbie Kirk—Graphic Design

Introduction

The life of the apostle Peter is one of divine turnaround. His life is God's way of infusing hope into the most hopeless situation. If you are human, then you have made mistakes. Our mistakes can be a prelude to our miracles. I have been in ministry for thirty years, and I have watched God use horrific mistakes for his glory. When we reach toward perfection, we fall short more often than not. As a pastor and family counselor, I have seen people rise from victims to victors. Serious situations, such as murder, molestation, domestic violence, and addictions, have been used by God to bring people to a saving knowledge of Jesus Christ. Our society is obsessed with success. We should all strive to do our best with the time we are allotted on earth. I contend that many of our success stories are more grace gifts than rags to riches. Listen to King David's testimony:

> [67]Before I was afflicted I went astray: but now have I kept thy word. [68] Thou art good, and doest good; teach me thy statutes. [69] The proud have forged a lie against me: but I will keep thy precepts with my whole heart. [70] Their heart is as fat as grease; but I delight in thy law. [71] It is good for me that I have been afflicted; that I might learn thy statutes. (Psalm 119:67–71)

A. Louis Patterson of the Mount Corinth Baptist Church of Houston, Texas, is fond of saying, "If what happens to you is not fatal, then it is not final, and God can use it to make you fruitful."

In *The Peter Paradox*, I examine the life and ministry of the disciple Peter through a series of sermons I preached at the Pilgrim Baptist Church in San Mateo, California, where I serve as senior pastor. God used Peter's mistakes to form him into a "rock" for Christ. I believe that we can learn principles from his life to help us mature in Christ.

Renowned leadership expert John C. Maxwell gives an acronym for mistakes in his book, *Failing Forward*, that he says helped him keep mistakes in perspective.

> Messages that give us feedback about life.
> Interruptions that should cause us to reflect and think.

Signposts that direct us to the right path.
Tests that push us toward greater maturity.
Awakenings that keep us in the game mentally.
Keys that we can use to unlock the next door of opportunity.
Explorations that let us journey where we have never been before.
Statements about our development and progress.

Often it is our response to life's difficulties and not the difficulties themselves that determine whether we become bitter or better. Why do some people experience a setback and grow, while others decide to cave in? In the final analysis, it is God's grace and goodness, but I believe that our choices also come into play. As we study Peter's life, we can learn from him to grow through life or simply go through life. Ultimately, this is a book about hope. Millions of men and women sit in prison cells every day. Even more make weekly visits to hospitals hoping the news is positive. Add the victims of various forms of abuse. Do not leave out the couples that thought their marriages would last a lifetime and are in the midst of separations and divorces.

It is encouraging to witness numerical growth in many churches. However, an increase in numbers does not mean an increase in mature believers. Why are so many modern believers marked by immaturity? Warren Wiersbe gives us his insight: "Maturity takes patience." We deceive ourselves when we think that we can grow up in Christ overnight. It is the training we receive from our mistakes that ushers us toward maturity.

The good news of the Gospel is that God can transform our mistakes into miracles.

Peter's Problem

♦

Text: Mark 14:1, 27–31, 70–72

After two days was the feast of the Passover, and of unleavened bread: and the chief priests and the scribes sought how they might take him by craft, and put him to death. (Mark 14:1)

[27] And Jesus saith unto them, All ye shall be offended because of me this night: for it is written, I will smite the shepherd, and the sheep shall be scattered. [28] But after that I am risen, I will go before you into Galilee. [29] But Peter said unto him, Although all shall be offended, yet will not I. [30] And Jesus saith unto him, Verily I say unto thee, That this day, even in this night, before the cock crow twice, thou shalt deny me thrice. [31] But he spake the more vehemently, If I should die with thee, I will not deny thee in any wise. Likewise also said they all. (Mark 14:27–31)

[70] And he denied it again. And a little after, they that stood by said again to Peter, Surely thou art one of them: for thou art a Galilean, and thy speech agreeth thereto. [71] But he began to curse and to swear, saying, I know not this man of whom ye speak. [72] And the second time the cock crew. And Peter called to mind the word that Jesus said unto him, Before the cock crow twice, thou shalt deny me thrice. And when he thought thereon, he wept. (Mark 14:70–72)

Peter's Problem
Text: Mark 14:1, 27–31, 70–72

1. Passover Plot

    a.   Defection

    b.   Denial

    c.   Death

2. Peter's Problem

    a.   Self-exalting

    b.   Sought explanation

    c.   Stood with enemy

3. Peter's Pain

    a.   Wrong place

    b.   Wrong people

    c.   Wrong language

Conclusion: His Pain…Our Gain

On January 9, 1969, Joe Namath played in Super Bowl III. He was called Broadway Joe because he was flashy, boastful, and lived large. In the game, the Baltimore Colts with Johnny Unitas and Lenny Moore were heavy favorites. Broadway Joe did something that was unheard of in that day...he came out on national television and guaranteed a victory. He was criticized for his guarantee, but he not only led the Jets to victory but was also voted MVP!

In our text today, Peter, one of the disciples of Jesus, guaranteed a victory. Jesus told them in the Upper Room that one of his own would defect from the group and betray him. Peter stands up and makes his guarantee to Jesus: "If everyone else denies you, I never will. I guarantee you that I will not only go to jail with you, I will die with you." Jesus tells Peter, "Before the rooster crows tonight, you will have denied me three times." But Peter says it again, "Lord you must not have heard me the first time I said it. If every one else falls away, I never will." Peter said something along the lines of, "You can deposit that in the bank. I guarantee it." (Matthew 26:35)

We are told in Mark 14:1, that the priests and scribes had a plot at Passover to kill Jesus. Passover is a Jewish celebration remembering the miraculous deliverance from slavery in Egypt.

Passover first began when Moses was sent to Pharaoh to tell him to release God's people from bondage. Pharaoh refused to let the people go. God sent nine plagues to get him to see the light, but he hardened his heart even more. In the tenth and final plague, God was going to destroy the firstborn children of all of Egypt if he did not let his people go. Still Pharaoh refused. God told Moses to have the Israelites put some blood over the door of each home, and, when the death angel came by and saw the blood, he would "pass over" that house. The children of Israel were set free that night, and from then until now, the Jews celebrate Passover.

The religious leaders made a Passover plot that, as soon as the celebration was over, they were going to kill Jesus. Now we are in the Upper Room, and Jesus tells them that one of them will defect from the group and betray him.

Defection:

It has been an unsolved mystery as to why Judas betrayed the Lord. He walked with him, heard him preach, and saw him teach. Judas saw the miracles, the healings, and even witnessed at least two people brought back from death. Yet, he defected from the Lord for thirty pieces of silver. Every person who sits under teaching and preaching must be doers of the Word and not hearers only. It is important for all of us, young and old, to make sure that the Word gets in us, so we do not end up like Judas, losing our soul while sitting at the feet of Jesus.

While they were in the Upper Room, Jesus shared with them his last meal, the Last Supper. He took bread and wine and gave it to them and told of his pending death. "I will strike the shepherd, and the sheep will be scattered." (Mark 14:27b) This was the prophecy that was fulfilled.

Denial:

Jesus is saying, "The only way for you to enter into a permanent covenant with my Father is that I become your permanent Passover. I want to fix it so that you will only have to celebrate me!" (If we truly believed this, then Easter would never be about fancy clothes and bunnies, and Christmas would not be about gifts and Santa Claus.) Peter then gives his guarantee: "If everyone else falls away I won't. I promise you I will go to jail or the grave, but I won't let you down." Jesus then tells him that before the night is over, he will deny him three times.

Peter's Problem:

I want us to look at Peter's problem together because there is a little bit of Peter in all of us.

1. His first problem is that he is self-exalting. He is full of himself and not full of God. He uses the word *I* three times. In Mark 14:29, "*I* will not scatter." In Mark 14:31, he says, "If it means my death *I* will not deny you" (italics added for emphasis). That is his guarantee. Whenever we sin, the letter I is in the middle of it. Pride always causes us to fall away.

2. The second problem that Peter had was that he would not ask the Lord to clarify what he was saying. He never said, "Lord what do you mean by us being offended? I don't understand. Could you explain it a little more for us?" In case you think that I am overstating the problem, look at another occasion:

    [20] Then charged he his disciples that they should tell no man that he was the Christ. [21] From that time forth began Jesus to shew unto his disciples, how that he must go unto Jerusalem, and suffer many things of the elders and chief priests and scribes, and be killed, and be raised again the third day. [22] Then Peter took him, and began to rebuke him, saying, "Be it far from thee, Lord: this shall not be unto thee." [23] But he turned, and said unto Peter, "Get thee behind me, Satan: thou

art an offence unto me: for thou savourest not the things that be of God, but those that be of men." (Matthew 16:20–23)

Many of us have had God speak to us in sermons, Sunday school classes, Bible studies, conferences, and our own devotions. What he says to us is clear, but we don't really hear him. At church, we hear announcements; it is amazing that something can be announced for several weeks, and after the event, someone will say that they didn't know about it!

3. Peter's third problem is that he stood too close to the enemy. In times of testing we need to surround ourselves with positive people. The company we keep will either hinder us or help us when our trials come. Let me ask you this question: Are your closest friends saved? Do you have bosom buddies in Christ? When you hang out, is it with people that have the same value system as you?

When you look at the Gospels, every time that Jesus did something significant, he took Peter, James, and John. When he healed certain hard cases, he took Peter, James, and John. On the Mount of Transfiguration, he took Peter, James, and John. In the Garden of Gethsemane, he took Peter, James, and John. Now Peter is following the Lord to his trial, and he is all by himself. Why didn't he follow the example of Jesus and take James and John with him?

Peter's Pain:

We have looked at the Passover plot. We have discussed Peter's problem. Now let's learn from his pain. The high priest was interrogating Jesus (verse 60), and he asked Jesus if he was the Christ, the Son of the blessed. I am so glad that the Lord did not deny who he was. Even when we deny him by our thoughts and actions, he will not deny himself. "I am who I am." They began to spit on him, slap him, and beat him down. (Mark 14:65)

Meanwhile, Peter is watching the action from under the porch. **He is in the wrong place.** He is not in prayer as the Lord instructed him to be, but he is peeping from under the porch, warming himself by a fire. One of the high priest's servants saw Peter and said he was a disciple of Jesus. Peter denied it and said he did not know what she was talking about. Another servant saw him and said that he was one of them. He denied again that he knew the Lord. A third time he was pointed out by the Lord's enemies, and he denied a third time by swearing a curse on himself. He said, "I guarantee you that I don't know Jesus." It was only that morning that Peter guaranteed that he would go to jail or even die for the Lord.

"If everyone else denies you, I never will." It turned out that he was the only one that denied him in this way. After he said it the third time, he recalled what the Lord said, and he wept.

In the midst of his weeping, he learned a lesson from pain that self-confidence could not teach him.

His pain was a blessing. How many of you know that God has to allow us to hurt before he can help us? C.S. Lewis once said, "In pleasure God whispers, but in pain he shouts."

Peter's pain:

1. Clarified his purpose

2. Taught him how to pray

3. Led to his spiritual progress

4. Taught him to stand on the promises

He learned that weeping may endure for a night, but joy comes in the morning.

> For his anger endureth but a moment; in his favour is life: weeping may endure for a night, but joy cometh in the morning. (Psalm 30:5)

Look at the text in Mark closely; there is a shout in the midst of the problems and the pain. It's in Mark 14:28: "After I am risen, I will meet you in Galilee." Thank God that he knows all about us, and he still has plans for us. Even when we fail, he won't throw us away.

Jesus said, "I must die in order to rise. I must suffer in order to be glorified. I will be your permanent Passover. I must shed my blood for not only your sins but for the sins of the whole world. I will fix it so that all anyone has to do is put my blood on them. Put my blood on your life. Put some blood on your marriage. Put some blood on your children. Put some blood on your business. Go ahead. Put some blood on your dreams. Put some blood on your sick body. When the enemy comes, he will have to pass over you. I must die. I must be buried. Here is my guarantee. I will rise again."

He is the only one that can guarantee a guarantee.

> If you confess your sins, I guarantee a cleansing.
> If you call me, I guarantee an answer.
> If you walk in the spirit, I guarantee you will not fall to your flesh.
> If you study God's word, I guarantee that you will grow.
> I guarantee you that no weapon formed against you shall prosper.

"Come to me all you that labor and are heavy laden, count on me and I will give you rest." (Matthew 11:28) "I will never leave you nor forsake you." (Hebrews 13:5c) Count on it. I love you. I will take care of you.

I have tried him, and I've learned that I can count on Jesus. Can you count on him? I know you can!

Discussion Questions

1. Is Peter's problem based on his feelings of inferiority or superiority?

2. Do you think Peter's personal exaltation was intentional?

3. Have you ever experienced being in the wrong place at the wrong time?

4. How much did Peter's temper play into his problem? (See John 18:10–11).

5. Has zealousness ever caused a problem for you?

6. Is humility a strength or weakness for you?

7. When you experience pain, does it clarify or cloud your purpose?

Peter's Pardon

✦

Text: Mark 16:1–7

[1] And when the sabbath was past, Mary Magdalene, and Mary the mother of James, and Salome, had bought sweet spices, that they might come and anoint him. [2] And very early in the morning the first day of the week, they came unto the sepulchre at the rising of the sun. [3] And they said among themselves, Who shall roll us away the stone from the door of the sepulchre? [4] And when they looked, they saw that the stone was rolled away: for it was very great. [5] And entering into the sepulchre, they saw a young man sitting on the right side, clothed in a long white garment; and they were affrighted. [6] And he saith unto them, Be not affrighted: Ye seek Jesus of Nazareth, which was crucified: he is risen; he is not here: behold the place where they laid him. [7] But go your way, tell his disciples and Peter that he goeth before you into Galilee: there shall ye see him, as he said unto you.

Title: Peter's Pardon
Text Mark 16:1–7

Peter's Past:

    a.   Remembered

    b.   Repented

    c.   Restored

Peter's Potential:

    a.   Satan knows your value

    b.   Savior knows your heart

    c.   Sin has no exemptions

Peter's Pardon:

    a.   Resurrection is an invitation

    b.   Resurrection is inclusive

    c.   Resurrection is a celebration

Conclusion: Pardon Party

Peter wanted to be the Joe Namath of the disciples and guarantee that if every-one else denied Jesus, he would not. However, he denied Jesus three times and wept bitterly. (Mark 14:72)

Peter had two problems. He had a problem with pride, and he had a problem listening to what Jesus said to him. (Whenever we have a hard head and a hard heart, we invite trouble. The surest way to let God down is to exalt yourself.)

Let's Review Peter's Problems:

1. He exalted himself: Peter was full of himself and not full of God. He used the word *I* three times. If everyone else fails you, *I won't, I won't, I won't*—but he did.

2. He didn't seek an explanation: When Jesus said that all will be offended because of him, Peter should have asked for an explanation. When God tells us something that we do not understand, we had better ask him what he means and not assume that what we thought we heard is what God actually said.

3. He ended up in a lot of pain: As a result of Peter's overconfidence and self-assurance, he denied the Lord just as he said he would not do. When Peter realized what he had done, he wept bitterly.

Pardon illustration:

Robert Blake, who played Detective Beretta on TV, was on trial for the murder of his wife. After a long agonizing trial, he was found not guilty. The look on his face was the look of a person who had been pardoned. When Scott Peterson was found guilty of the murder of his wife, Laci, and unborn son, Connor, do you remember the look on his face? It was the look of one found guilty with no hope of pardon.

The prayer in the Garden of Gethsemane was prayed. Judas betrayed the Lord. Pilate washed his hands of the whole matter. The crowd shouted in deafen-ing tones, "Crucify him. Crucify him. Crucify him." They led him up a steep hill shaped like a skull, perfect to die on. They spat on him and pushed sharp thorns into his head. They offered him cheap, bitter wine to dull his pain. They pierced his side and hammered heavy one-pound nails into his hands and feet. He died in pain so great that the human mind cannot fathom it. He did not die for his sin but for the sins of the whole world. Yes, your sin and mine. He said that no man could take his life, but he laid it down voluntarily. He died. He died such a violent death that nature could not stand to watch. The sun refused to shine, and even the moon is said to have dripped blood. The earth quaked so violently that it surpassed the Richter scale. Joseph of Arimathaea begged for Jesus's body and laid it in a new tomb.

The women came to the tomb early in the morning. On their way, they remembered that a huge stone used as a Roman seal was placed in front of the tomb to secure it. While they wondered who would roll the massive stone away, they looked up and the stone had already been moved.

That's enough to shout about right there—just when you wonder how God will make a way, you discover that the way has already been made.

A young man, an angel sent by God to supervise the Resurrection told the women that they did not need to be alarmed. They must have been full of emotions, part of which were probably fear and amazement.

> And he saith unto them, "Be not affrighted: Ye seek Jesus of Nazareth, which was crucified: he is risen; he is not here: behold the place where they laid him." (Mark 16:6)

> Look at where they laid him but look at it again for he is not dead but alive.

> But go your way, tell his disciples *and Peter* that he goeth before you into Galilee: there shall ye see him, as he said unto you. (Mark 16:7)

Peter's Past:

The good news is that the angel singles out Peter. He is still part of the group. His denial broke the fellowship but not the relationship.

Jesus said, "I will meet you in Galilee." (Mark 16:7) The truth of that promise still stands. The promises that God makes before we make our mistakes still stand after we make them. When Peter remembered his overconfidence and repented of his denial, the Lord restored him.

Brothers and sisters, I am convinced that most of us are paralyzed by our past. Some things we have done we wish we had not done. Other things that we did not do we wish we could have another chance to do. We are caught in the trap of would have, could have, and should have. The twin assassins of guilt and shame haunt us. Many people live in self-made garrisons of past failures. Parents feel that if they had done more than their son or daughter would not have turned to drugs. A spouse laments that had he or she made a greater sacrifice perhaps their marriage would have lasted. Consider the life of the apostle Paul. He surely reflected on the murders to which he gave consent. Did not Moses think of the Egyptian that he slew? We must believe that God is present even when we make mistakes or we will live a life of regret.

> [8] If we say that we have no sin, we deceive ourselves, and the truth is not in us. [9] If we confess our sins, he is faithful and just to forgive us our sins, and to cleanse us from all unrighteousness. (1 John 1:8–9)

Peter's Potential:

Let me say it again: whatever God tells us in the light still stands when we are in the dark. Jesus told all of the disciples that he would go to Jerusalem and suffer and be crucified, but that on the third day he would rise from the dead. Not one of the disciples understood the teaching! Spending three years under Jesus' tutelage did not guarantee that Peter understood what he heard.

This hit home when I asked members at our midweek Bible study about the past Sunday's sermon, and no one remembered the title, the main points, or the great quotes that I had preached two days earlier. Then I remembered that oftentimes, while my mother dispensed her wisdom for me, I was looking at the ceiling. Now years later, I get it. Let's not be too hard on ourselves and others when we do not get it right away. The truth takes time to get past our defenses: our hard heads and our hard hearts.

God knows our potential. We get stuck looking at where we are, but God knows where we can go. God saw in Peter a winner, not a loser. God saw in Peter not just someone who would let him down, but someone who would one day lift him up. Just as God knows our potential, Satan knows our value. Satan would not spend hell's energy to keep you in bondage if he did not know your great potential when you surrender everything to Jesus. Satan knows that once you let Jesus control your heart, you will be an awesome instrument in God's hand. It does not matter who you are but whose you are.

The difference between Judas and Peter is that Judas let Satan enter him:

> Then entered Satan into Judas surnamed Iscariot, being of the number of the twelve. (Luke 22:3)

Satan desired Peter but Jesus prayed for him.

> [31] And the Lord said, "Simon, Simon, behold, Satan hath desired to have you, that he may sift you as wheat: [32] But I have prayed for thee, that thy faith fail not: and when thou art converted, strengthen thy brethren." (Luke 22:31–32)

The thing that makes sin so powerful is that it is so deceitful. Everyone thinks that it will not slay them. "I can handle it. Let me live my own life. You had your fun; let me have mine. Give me some space. If I make mistakes, I will deal with them. Leave me alone." We say it to God every time we turn our back on his Word. We say it to God when we refuse to commit our lives to him. When Satan hears us say it, he knows that we are not far from failure. The Lord saw in Judas the potential for betrayal, but he saw in Peter the potential for preaching; so Jesus prayed for him. The Lord really knows our hearts, and we should pray that what he sees in our hearts is not betrayal.

Peter's Pardon:

We see in the Resurrection an invitation. It is an invitation to the "whosoever will" group. It states that the God of the Resurrection loves you. Your sins, though they are many, are nailed to the cross. Even though your sins are as scarlet, Jesus promises to wash you whiter than snow. (Isaiah 1:18)

It is an invitation to come as you are and not wait until you think you are worthy. It is inclusive. No one is left out. You have to decline the invitation to be left out. God will not change your heart if you do not really want to be changed. You have a right to be condemned like Judas or pardoned like Peter. It is your choice. No one can choose this great salvation for you. You alone have the key in your heart that, when inserted in the door covered by the shed blood of Jesus, will admit you to heaven.

The Resurrection is a celebration. It is a celebration of God's commitment to us through Christ. There is a party that heaven is throwing. It is a pardon party. The guest list is long, but there is always room for more.

Party list:

Adam and Eve will be there representing those who made bad choices.
Noah will be there representing those who got drunk.
Abraham will be there representing those who lied.
Sarah will be there representing those who laughed at God's promises.
Jonah will be there representing preachers who did not want everybody to be saved.
Moses will be there representing reformed murderers.
Mary, Martha, and Lazarus will be there.
Paul and Silas are on the list.
Matthew, Mark, Luke, and John will surely be there.

I see housewives, missionaries, and faithful laypeople.
People from every race, color, and creed.

Jesus has pardon power. Have you felt it? Can you feel it? Pardon power. The question is, Will you be at the pardon party? If you plan to be there, let me hear you say, "Party over here!" I see Jesus sitting on his throne:

King of Kings
Lord of Lords
Alpha and Omega
Crown him, crown him, bring forth the royal diadem, and crown him Lord of all.
Thank you, Jesus. Thank you, Lord. God, I thank you that I have a mother in heaven and one day I will join her!

Discussion Questions

1. Do you have a problem forgiving others?

2. Do you have a problem accepting forgiveness from others?

3. Does your past paralyze you?

4. How do you know if you are reaching your God-given potential?

5. Are you experiencing resurrection power in your daily life?

6. What does it mean to you to be pardoned by God?

7. Is confession of known sin easy for you? (See 1 John 1:9).

Peter's Priorities

✦

John 21:3–7, 10, 15–18

[3] Simon Peter saith unto them, I go a fishing. They say unto him, We also go with thee. They went forth, and entered into a ship immediately; and that night they caught nothing. [4] But when the morning was now come, Jesus stood on the shore: but the disciples knew not that it was Jesus. [5] Then Jesus saith unto them, Children, have ye any meat? They answered him, No. [6] And he said unto them, Cast the net on the right side of the ship, and ye shall find. They cast therefore, and now they were not able to draw it for the multitude of fishes. [7] Therefore that disciple whom Jesus loved saith unto Peter, It is the Lord. Now when Simon Peter heard that it was the Lord, he girt his fisher's coat unto him, (for he was naked,) and did cast himself into the sea. (John 21:3–7)

Jesus saith unto them, Bring of the fish which ye have now caught. (John 21:10)

[15] So when they had dined, Jesus saith to Simon Peter, Simon, son of Jonas, lovest thou me more than these? He saith unto him, Yea, Lord; thou knowest that I love thee. He saith unto him, Feed my lambs. [16] He saith to him again the second time, Simon, son of Jonas, lovest thou me? He saith unto him, Yea, Lord; thou knowest that I love thee. He saith unto him, Feed my sheep. [17] He saith unto him the third time, Simon, son of Jonas, lovest thou me? Peter was grieved because he said unto him the third time, Lovest thou me? And he said unto him, Lord, thou knowest all things; thou knowest that I love thee. Jesus saith unto him, Feed my sheep. [18] Verily, verily, I say unto thee, When thou wast young, thou girdedst thyself, and walkedst whither thou wouldest: but when thou shalt be old, thou shalt stretch forth thy hands, and

another shall gird thee, and carry thee whither thou wouldest not. (John 21:15–18)

Peter's Priorities
Text: John 21:3–7, 10, 15–18

1. Peter's Decision:

    a.   Return to his past

    b.   Return to his problem

    c.   Return to his pain

2. Peter's Defeat:

    a.   Unsuccessful

    b.   Unrecognizing

    c.   Unclothed

3. Peter's Discipline:

    a.   Admit your love

    b.   Amount of your love

    c.   Act on your love

Conclusion: Follow me

Good parents, good principals, good teachers, good pastors and preachers, good physicians, good planners, good presidents and politicians, good people in general have one thing in common: they pay attention to priorities. They make the main thing the main thing. They believe in business before pleasure, work before play, homework before TV, chores before PlayStation, bill-paying before mall-shopping, and cash before credit.

Having priorities means putting first things first—making sure that the main thing remains the main thing. This is a valuable lesson in all areas of your life because your success will depend on your priorities. How much you know and grow will depend on your priorities. If you keep your priorities in order, you will go further in life than the person who may be smarter than you, stronger than you, and even wealthier than you. In your walk with God, priorities are important. The person that grows in the Lord learns that the Christian life works best when you place God first in all that you do. The Scriptures were given to make us wise. The consequences of our choices will reflect in the quality of our lives. The wisdom in Proverbs is not only good advice; it also makes good sense.

> [5] Trust in the Lord with all thine heart; and lean not unto thine own understanding. [6] In all thy ways acknowledge him, and he shall direct thy paths.
> [7] Be not wise in thine own eyes: fear the Lord, and depart from evil.
> [8] It shall be health to thy navel, and marrow to thy bones. [9] Honour the Lord with thy substance, and with the firstfruits of all thine increase: [10] So shall thy barns be filled with plenty, and thy presses shall burst out with new wine. (Proverbs 3:5–10)

Did you notice that the right priorities influence your soul, your health, and your wealth?

After his Resurrection, Jesus told the angel to tell the women at the tomb to tell the disciples and Peter to meet him in Galilee. Don't miss the importance of having a disposition that will allow people to give you advice. Some people have the attitude that you cannot tell them anything, and usually that includes the Lord as well. Peter became impatient during the time between the command to go to Galilee and actually meeting the Lord Jesus. The time between God, giving us a promise and fulfilling that promise can be a difficult time. Most of us are impatient.

> But they that wait upon the Lord shall renew their strength; they shall mount up with wings as eagles; they shall run, and not be weary; and they shall walk, and not faint. (Isaiah 40:31)

In her book, *You're Late Again, Lord!* Karon Goodman writes that none of us like to spend time in God's waiting room. The truth is that we don't like to wait in traffic, in bank lines and grocery lines, or on other people. It comes as no surprise that we don't like to wait—even on God.

Peter's Decision:

Peter grew tired of waiting for Jesus to show up in Galilee. He figured that he had waited long enough. After all, the other disciples claimed to have already seen Him. Peter may have joined doubting Thomas. He decided to go fishing. His decision was more than an activity to pass the time. It represented a return to his old life. In Luke 5:10, Jesus told him that he was to become a "fisher of men." Peter may have left his old job physically, but he still had it in his heart.

Until we remove some things from our hearts, we cannot move forward in our lives. Seven of the disciples are listed: that means that seven of the twelve disciples were fishermen. Why? Fishermen were tough, patient, hardworking people. They were committed, courageous, and confident. Their lives depended upon them going out into deep water every day. You could not fish one day a week and survive. Just as you cannot live off a single Sunday helping of spiritual nourishment and expect to grow. Peter makes a poor decision and influences the other six to disobey God along with him. Most sinners are not content with sinning alone. They want partners in their crimes against God.

They fished all night and caught nothing. This is déjà vu for Peter. He had this same experience two years earlier but had forgotten a valuable lesson. Without God, you can do nothing. Without him, you will surely fail. Just as Peter felt the pain that came with denying Jesus, he now feels the pain that comes from getting ahead of Jesus. It is never a waste of time to wait on God, but it is always a waste of time to get in a hurry and get ahead of God.

Lesson from the Oyster

> Expensive pearls are made in an unusual way. A grain of sand gets in an oyster's shell. The oyster tries to remove it. The more it works to remove

it, the more friction is created and over a long period of time, a pearl is made. The difference between a cheap pearl and an expensive one is how long the sand stays in the shell with the pearl. The longer it stays, the more valuable the pearl. The same is true in the spiritual realm. The longer you wait, the greater the blessing God has in store for you. If you try to rush the process, you cheapen what God is trying to make out of your life!

Peter's Defeat:

The magnificent seven fished all night and caught nothing. The next morning, Jesus stood on the shore. Could it be that they were only one day ahead of Jesus? What a difference a day can make. The job you quit, the relationship you ended, the class you dropped—all could have been different had you not been bitten by the bug of impatience. How many of us have discovered that haste makes waste?

Jesus has a great sense of humor. I believe that he watched them all night struggling with empty nets. Frustration must have set in as the night crept on. Waiting and watching, waiting and watching, waiting and watching…nothing! Impatient Peter ended up waiting anyway.

Have you ever been driving on the freeway and someone passes you weaving in and out of traffic in a hurry? Farther up the road, there they are, pulled over by the highway patrol. Wherever they were going, they are late for sure. When we get ahead of God, we guarantee failure.

I can imagine that Jesus would have asked them, What did you boys catch? Did you have a good night? Speak up I can't hear you…nothing? Unscriptural activities lead to unfruitful results. The surest way to fail is to get ahead of God or to not consult God at all. You will never save time. You will always waste time. In other words, whenever we go without orders, we end up without blessings. Self-leading is a waste of time.

The disciples were well-known for their lack of faith and vision. They did not catch any fish nor did they recognize Jesus.

> But when the morning was now come, Jesus stood on the shore: but the disciples knew not that it was Jesus. (John 21:4)

Look at the disciples—they are unsuccessful, they are unable to recognize Jesus, and Peter is unclothed! Jesus asks the question, "How well have you done without me?" For those of you that are still running your own life, how well have *you* done? I am not talking about money. How well is your soul? How much peace do you have in your life? Do you have any joy? If you are walking closely with the Lord, how well are you doing? Can you testify that you have been blessed by the Lord? Are you much better off in all areas of your life since you met Jesus?

Peter's Discipline:

Jesus told Peter to fish on the right side. You and I can be mere feet away from a miracle. But that might as well be a million miles if we are not where God wants us to be. Notice that the fish were there all of the time, but Peter and the disciples could not catch them. (When will we learn that we can do more with God than without him?)

When they finally recognized that it was the Lord, they were too embarrassed to say anything. Notice that they caught 153 fish—fish so large that they filled the boat. I believe that the number is given to show that you will catch bigger fish and have greater success when you obey God. Notice that together they could not haul the fish in, but Jesus gave Peter miraculous power to haul them in all by himself. Again, no matter who you are, when you hook up with Jesus, you will become a dynamic duo, a terrific twosome. Here is the shout. When they got to the shore, Jesus had fish and bread already cooked and waiting! Don't miss the miracle. God has waiting for you all the things that you are killing yourself trying to accomplish on your own.

> But seek ye first the kingdom of God, and his righteousness; and all these things shall be added unto you. (Matthew 6:33)

Conclusion:

"Peter, look at the fish. Peter, look at your fellow disciples. Peter, look at your boat. Peter, look at your equipment. Peter, look at yourself. Do you love me more than all of these?" Peter says, "Lord, you know I love you." (John 21:15) Let's look closely at the words.

Jesus uses the word *agape.* Peter uses *phileo.* There is a difference. Do you love me with all of your heart? Lord, you know that I love you a lot. Do you love me more than anyone or anything? Lord, you know that I am crazy for you.

It's like saying to a man, "Do you love me more than the National Football League, National Basketball Association, National Hockey League, your car, and your job put together?"

To a woman, "Do you love me more than your family, job, shopping, a wedding shower or Sunday brunch with your best friend?"

To a young person, "Do you love me more than fashion, fads, toys, peers, music, and TV?"

To everyone, "How much do you love me? Do you love me enough to put me first? Do you love me more than other people? Do you love me more than your plans? Do you love me more than your money? Will you serve me? Will you get to know my Word? Will you get in ministry?" "Follow me before disease sets in. Follow me before disability comes. Follow me before death comes. Follow me."

Tell the Lord that where he leads, you will follow. Tell him that you will go all the way. Tell him that you need him and love him. Go ahead and tell him!

Discussion Questions

1. What was Peter really holding onto?

2. Do you have problems setting priorities?

3. Is decision making easy for you?

4. Do you stick with decisions after you have made them?

5. List your life's priorities.

6. Are your priorities in line with God's priorities?

7. What changes do you need to make?

Peter's Power Source

✦

Text: Acts 2:36–41

[36] Therefore let all the house of Israel know assuredly, that God hath made that same Jesus, whom ye have crucified, both Lord and Christ.

[37] Now when they heard this, they were pricked in their heart, and said unto Peter and to the rest of the apostles, Men and brethren, what shall we do? [38] Then Peter said unto them, Repent, and be baptized every one of you in the name of Jesus Christ for the remission of sins, and ye shall receive the gift of the Holy Ghost. [39] For the promise is unto you, and to your children, and to all that are afar off, even as many as the Lord our God shall call. [40] And with many other words did he testify and exhort, saying, Save yourselves from this untoward generation.

[41] Then they that gladly received his word were baptized: and the same day there were added unto them about three thousand souls.

Peter's Power Source
Text: Acts 2:36–41

1. Peter the Person

    a. His change

2. Peter the Preacher

    a. His courage

3. Peter's Power Source

    a. His Christ-centeredness

Conclusion: I Can

Introduction

Imagine the NCAA championship game: Illinois versus North Carolina. The Edward Jones Arena is packed, and the referee is ready for the tip-off. But something's missing: there is no basketball.

Super Bowl XXXIX, Jacksonville, Florida. They are ready for the kickoff, but something is missing: there is no football.

You just received your favorite game—Xbox or PlayStation. But something's missing: there's no game cartridge. You are all set to shop, but something's missing: there is not a 50 Percent Off sign anywhere. How about this: You are starving, and the table is set with fine china. But something's missing: there is nothing in the pots. You are sixty-five, all set to retire, and something's missing: there is no Social Security money left—that's not funny, is it?

If you take an honest look at the world today, you do not have to be a genius to conclude that something is missing. Look at our families, our school systems, our political infighting, our health care system, and the increase in violent crime. Something is missing. When we take an honest look at the worldwide church today, an honest look at our personal lives—I said an honest look—most of us would have to admit that something's missing.

The text describes the day of Pentecost. Fifty days after the Resurrection of Jesus, we see a church that is on fire spiritually. The preacher preaches in one language, and the Holy Spirit translates the language so that everyone hears the Gospel of Jesus Christ in his or her birth language. People from sixteen different countries—representing every cultural group under heaven—all participating in the same service. Miracles were happening on a daily basis. People were saved, healed, and delivered on a daily basis.

Peter the Person:

A close look at the program tells us that Peter is the preacher of the hour. Peter? Yes, Peter, who just fifty days earlier denied that he even knew the Lord and, for good measure, threw in a few choice curse words. Remember he returned to his old job of fishing because Jesus did not show up soon enough to suit him.

Peter is a reminder that God uses imperfect people. When you let God down, let your family down, and even let yourself down, your life does not have to be over. God is in the recycling business. The good news of the Gospel of Jesus Christ is that God will take misfits and fit them for his Kingdom.

Before you exclude yourself from that category, let me remind you that the Bible teaches that no one is righteous apart from Christ. All of our personal righteousness is as filthy rags in God's sight. Romans 3:23 does not say that ya'll have sinned, it says all have sinned and come short of God's glory. The fact that God chose Peter to give the first sermon after Easter should be an encouragement that whatever you have been through, if it was not fatal, then it is not final, and it can still be fruitful.

I want us to understand Peter's transformation.

1. He used to carry a weapon (all you weapon carriers, say amen).

2. He used to curse (all you cursers, say amen).

3. He was full of himself (all you proud folk, say amen).

4. He thought he knew more than God Almighty (all you that are arrogant say amen).

5. He loved to fight (all the violent say amen).

6. He went to jail.

Peter the Preacher:

Just fifty days ago, Peter was a backslider. He kept falling down. He kept getting in God's way and in his own way. Jesus told them to get together and pray and wait for the promised Holy Spirit to come upon them.

> But ye shall receive power, after that the Holy Ghost is come upon you: and ye shall be witnesses unto me both in Jerusalem, and in all Judaea, and in Samaria, and unto the uttermost part of the earth. (Acts 1:8)

One hundred twenty believers in one place, on one accord, waited for ten days. Prayer and fasting was the only agenda. There was a sound from heaven: a rushing mighty wind that filled the house. Divided tongues appeared, as if fire were set on each of them. They were filled with the Holy Spirit and spoke with other tongues. Moses saw a fire in a bush; they had fire inside them.

Note the order:

1. One accord

2. One place

3. Prayed up

4. Filled with the Holy Spirit

5. Spoke in other tongues

6. Devout or holy folk

7. The tongues were evidence that it was from God

8. None of these steps can be left out

Even with the Holy Spirit's filling, there were still some people in the crowd that did not see the spiritual fire and did not catch it.

[12] And they were all amazed, and were in doubt, saying one to another, What meaneth this? [13] Others mocking said, These men are full of new wine. (Acts 2:12–13)

Even today, some people can be in worship, with the power of God everywhere, and they don't feel or change a thing. Peter stood up in Acts 1:15 and again in Acts 2:14. Peter is filled with God's spirit, and he is no longer the same person.

Listen to him quoting the Old Testament book of Joel:

[28] And it shall come to pass afterward, that I will pour out my spirit upon all flesh; and your sons and your daughters shall prophesy, your old men shall dream dreams, your young men shall see visions: [29] And also upon the servants and upon the handmaids in those days will I pour out my spirit. [30] And I will show wonders in the heavens and in the earth, blood, and fire, and pillars of smoke. [31] The sun shall be turned into darkness, and the moon into blood, before the great and the terrible day of the Lord come. [32] And it shall come to pass, that whosoever shall call on the name of the Lord shall be delivered: for in Mount Zion and in Jerusalem shall be deliverance, as the Lord hath said, and in the remnant whom the Lord shall call. (Joel 2:28–32)

Interpreting the meaning of the passage, he then recites Psalm 16:8–11:

[8] I have set the Lord always before me: because he is at my right hand, I shall not be moved. [9] Therefore my heart is glad, and my glory rejoiceth: my flesh also shall rest in hope. [10] For thou wilt not leave my soul in hell; neither wilt thou suffer thine Holy One to see corruption. [11] Thou wilt show me the path of life: in thy presence is fullness of joy; at thy right hand there are pleasures for evermore.

And then Psalm 110:1:

> A Psalm of David.

> The Lord said unto my Lord, Sit thou at my right hand, until I make thine enemies thy footstool.

Peter's Power Source

Peter had courage, conviction, and confidence. Fifty days ago, he was scared. Now he is bold. He tells the crowd that this same Jesus that they crucified and buried, God has raised from the dead. He has been exalted to the right hand of God. He is both Lord and Christ. Every knee must bow and every tongue must confess that he is Lord. He was crucified for their sins. They nailed him to the cross. They rejected his love and spurned his grace and mercy.

The audience was convicted of their sins; the Word of God stabbed them in their heart as a hot knife slashes through butter. What must we do? When God has control over you, you do not come to church and decide what you will or won't do. Your attitude is that *I* must do. I must be right. I must be saved. I must be filled with the Holy Spirit.

Our part:
1. Repent
2. Be baptized

God's part:
3. Forgive
4. Give us the Holy Spirit

The Holy Spirit is a surgeon. We all need surgery continuously. We all have weaknesses, but when we see ourselves as we really are, we must go under the knife of God's Word.

Let me make it plain. Surrender to Christ. Stop running your own life. Live by the Holy Bible. Let the Spirit of God take control of you, moment by moment, day by day. Notice, it was for everyone: men, women, and children.

In my hometown of Clarksville, Tennessee, God called three young men into the ministry at the ages of fourteen, sixteen, and nineteen. The nineteen-year-old is now twenty-one and is pastoring a growing church in Michigan; the other two are preaching at schools, in the streets, and conducting revivals. The book of Joel says that in the last days the Spirit will fall on everyone, and whosoever calls on the name of the Lord shall be saved.

Peter said that in order to be saved, you have to turn your life around and come to Jesus. He loves you. He cares about you. He hung on the cross for you.

He laid in a cold grave for three days for you, but God raised him up. Now you can be saved, changed, and restored.

Notice that those who received the Word gladly were baptized. I can see them saying, "Run some water, I can't wait." There were about sixty thousand people present that day in Jerusalem, and three thousand souls came to Christ. God will accept you today.

A schoolteacher in Rwanda, Central Africa, grew tired of his cold church and his empty spiritual life. He shut himself up for a week in his cottage for prayer and fasting. He came out a new man and started a revival that brought thousands to Christ. About the same time, God reached down into Chicago and touched an illiterate shoe salesman named Dwight L. Moody. Through God he started a church and a Sunday school and thousands were saved. They called Moody crazy because he would chase kids and bring them to church. History has shown over and over again that…

> If my people, which are called by my name, shall humble themselves, and pray, and seek my face, and turn from their wicked ways; then will I hear from heaven, and will forgive their sin, and will heal their land. (2 Chronicles 7:14)

Conclusion:

Can God's spirit fall again? Can God still change lives? Can God still convict sinners? Can God set a church on fire today? Can God work miracles? God can. God can save. God can heal. God can set free. When we let the Holy Spirit have his way, then we can become an "I can" people.

1. I can raise my children alone.

2. I can break bad habits.

3. I can improve my health.

4. I can get out of debt.

5. I can grow spiritually.

6. I can stop being mean and messy.

7. I can improve my marriage.

8. I can do all things through Christ.

Let the Holy Ghost into your life. He will save you, fill you, change you, seal you, dwell in you, lead you, guide you, anoint you, and appoint you. He prays, he speaks, he convicts, he converts, and he convinces. Let him in, let him in, and let him in today. He will give you a new mind, a new heart, a new tongue. Let him in.

Discussion Questions

1. How do you define power?

2. How do you use power?

3. Does it take courage to change?

4. How do you think power is abused?

5. If you had more power, how would you use it?

6. Do you allow the Holy Spirit to be your power source?

7. What did you learn from Peter in this message?

Peter's Power Source Part II

✦

Text: Acts 4:1–14

[1] And as they spake unto the people, the priests, and the captain of the temple, and the Sadducees, came upon them, [2] Being grieved that they taught the people, and preached through Jesus the resurrection from the dead. [3] And they laid hands on them, and put them in hold unto the next day: for it was now eventide. [4] Howbeit many of them which heard the word believed; and the number of the men was about five thousand.

[5] And it came to pass on the morrow, that their rulers, and elders, and scribes, [6] And Annas the high priest, and Caiaphas, and John, and Alexander, and as many as were of the kindred of the high priest, were gathered together at Jerusalem. [7] And when they had set them in the midst, they asked, By what power, or by what name, have ye done this? [8] Then Peter, filled with the Holy Ghost, said unto them, Ye rulers of the people, and elders of Israel, [9] If we this day be examined of the good deed done to the impotent man, by what means he is made whole; [10] Be it known unto you all, and to all the people of Israel, that by the name of Jesus Christ of Nazareth, whom ye crucified, whom God raised from the dead, even by him doth this man stand here before you whole. [11] This is the stone which was set at nought of you builders, which is become the head of the corner. [12] Neither is there salvation in any other: for there is none other name under heaven given among men, whereby we must be saved.

[13] Now when they saw the boldness of Peter and John, and perceived that they were unlearned and ignorant men, they marvelled; and they took knowledge of them, that they had been with Jesus. [14] And

beholding the man which was healed standing with them, they could say nothing against it.

Title: Peter's Power Source Part II
Text: Acts 4:1–14

1. Peter Shares His Faith with the People:

    A. Positive response

2. Peter Is Sent to Prison as a Form of Persecution:

    B. Preaches the Resurrection

3. Peter Stands Up in the Holy Spirit's Power:

    C. Presents his reason

    Closing arguments

    1. I have been changed

    2. The man has been changed

    3. Others have been changed

Peter Shares His Faith with the People:

Peter had to be on a spiritual high. A forty-year-old man paralyzed for many years is miraculously healed. (Acts 3) It happened in an instant. Peter and John were on their way to the temple to pray, and this paralyzed beggar shook his cup asking for a handout. Peter said, "Look on us, and the man looked, expecting an offering from him." Peter said, "I do not have any money, but what I do have, I give you in the name of Jesus Christ of Nazareth. Stand up and walk."(Acts 3:6-7) He took the man by his right hand, and his feet and ankles were healed. The man started shouting. The people began praising God. Peter did what every believer should do when God uses him or her: give the credit to whom it belongs.

The problem with some of us is that we think that Gods power is partly ours, and some of the credit belongs to us. Miracles are divine opportunities to share your faith. God healed this paralyzed man. In witnessing to the crowd, Peter extended God's mercy. We should never lose sight of the fact that grace and mercy draw people to Jesus. We specialize in condemnation but Jesus offers salvation. It is not too late to turn your life over to him.

Just as Peter was feeling the joy of the Lord, the priests, temple police, and the Sadducees swooped down on him. They were extremely angry about Peter's subject matter. Whenever God starts blessing, the devil starts messing. He preached the Resurrection of Jesus Christ, which means that we have victory.

The Sadducees were upset because they did not believe in the resurrection from the dead. The opponents of Christianity just could not stomach some things. They placed Peter and John in prison for sharing their faith. Peter is guilty of obeying Jesus. Satan was behind it all. We must remember that if obeying God gets you in trouble, then God will be present in the trouble.

Positive response:

The reason that we should be faithful in sharing our faith is found in verse four:

> Howbeit many of them which heard the word believed; and the number of the men was about five thousand. (Acts 4:4)

Whatever we experience because of telling people about Jesus is worth it. I would rather spend a lifetime in jail for preaching Christ than spend a day in the king's palace for keeping my mouth shut. Evidence against Peter:

Exhibits:

1 Soul winner (Acts 2:21)
2 Teacher/discipler (Acts 2:14)
3 Involved in the fellowship (Acts 2:42)
4 Lame man healed (Acts 3:2-8)
5 Boldness (Acts 3:13-17) (Acts 4:13)
6 Obedience (Acts 5:29)
7 A changed life (First and Second Peter)
8 Good works (Acts 3:1)

If you were charged with practicing Christianity, would there be enough evidence to convict you?

Peter Is Sent to Prison as a Form of Persecution:

The people of God seem to have difficulty handling persecution. We cannot handle it when we hear unkind remarks, see unwelcoming glares, or receive cold shoulders. We tend to fold, even when someone walks by and refuses to speak to us. That is usually enough to send us home. Peter demonstrates for us that the Holy Spirit's filling gives us the strength we need to face anyone or anything.

Peter is brought before the rulers, elders, scribes, Annas, Caiaphas, John, and Alexander. It seems that when we face opposition, we are outnumbered. We may be outnumbered in the natural but never in the supernatural. Here is an example of how God is present even though we may not be aware of his presence.

The story of Elisha's servant
Illustration:

[15] And when the servant of the man of God was risen early, and gone forth, behold, an host compassed the city both with horses and chariots. And his servant said unto him, Alas, my master! how shall we do? [16] And he answered, Fear not: for they that be with us are more than they that be with them. [17] And Elisha prayed, and said, Lord, I pray thee, open his eyes, that he may see. And the Lord opened the eyes of the young man; and he saw: and, behold, the mountain was full of horses and chariots of fire round about Elisha. (2 Kings 6:15–17)

Peter Stands Up in the Holy Spirit's Power:

Rulers asked Peter, "By whose name have you done this miracle?" Peter had courage, conviction, and confidence. Fifty days earlier, he would have cowered in fear. Now he is bold. "You nailed him to the cross. You spurned his love, grace, and mercy." Peter repeated the message of the Resurrection. "The man who stands before you was healed by Jesus, whom you crucified."(Acts 4:8-11) There is salvation in no other name.

You know his name don't you?

Author of my faith

Babe of Bethlehem

Chief shepherd

Door of the sheepfold

Emmanuel

Friend of sinners

God

Head of the church

Invincible

Jehovah

King of kings

Lord of lords

Messiah

Nobody like him

Only begotten son of the Father

Prince of peace

Quick to answer prayer

Resurrection

Soon to return

True vine

Unique

Valuable

Wonderful

eXcellent and exciting

Yield yourself to him

Zeal will set you on fire

There is healing in his name.

There is deliverance in his name.

There is salvation in his name.

There is blessing in his name.

I hear Peter saying, "Men, you are both judge and jury, so let me personalize my defense by giving you my testimony:

By faith I left my fishing business to follow Jesus. (Matthew 4:18-20)

By faith I said, 'You are the Christ, son of the living God.' (Matthew 16:16)

By faith I walked on water. (Matthew 14:28-29)

By faith I went to the tomb.(Luke 24:13)

By faith I was restored. (Mark 16:7)

By faith I am filled with his Spirit right now." (Acts 2:14)

He said, "I am not dressed like you, but I am saved. I am not as educated as you, but I am saved."

[26] For ye see your calling, brethren, how that not many wise men after the flesh, not many mighty, not many noble, are called: [27] But God hath chosen the foolish things of the world to confound the wise; and God hath chosen the weak things of the world to confound the things which are mighty; [28] And base things of the world, and things which are despised, hath God chosen, yea, and things which are not, to bring to nought things that are: [29] That no flesh should glory in his presence. (1 Cor. 1:26–29)

Closing Arguments:

Peter would say, "I want to close my defense by telling you that you can do whatever you want to do to me, but I will never deny my Lord again. You can take my life but you can't touch my testimony."

> And without controversy great is the mystery of godliness: God was manifest in the flesh, justified in the Spirit, seen of angels, preached unto the Gentiles, believed on in the world, received up into glory. (1 Timothy 3:16)

> [11] It is a faithful saying: For if we be dead with him, we shall also live with him: [12] If we suffer, we shall also reign with him: if we deny him, he also will deny us: [13] If we believe not, yet he abideth faithful: he cannot deny himself. (2 Timothy 2:11–13)

"I have been changed. The man that stands here with me has been changed. Five thousand others have been changed."

> "You judged my past, but my past has been nailed to the cross.
> You judged my lack of training, but he rose to give me power.
> You judged my mistakes, but he fixed my failures.
> You judged my ministry, but this healed man is proof.
> You commanded me to shut my mouth, but I can't help but to preach.
> You called me good for nothing, but that does not fit.
> You called me ignorant, but that does not fit.
> You called me an impostor, but that does not fit.
> You say I am a loser, but that does not fit."

Discussion Questions

1. Discuss your understanding of evangelism.

2. Do you share your faith on a regular basis?

3. Have you ever been persecuted for your faith?

4. How do you explain the change in Peter?

5. How important is it for you to pass your faith to friends and family?

6. Why do you think evangelism is a low priority for most Christians?

7. Why do you think evangelism is a low priority for most churches?

Peter's Power Source Part III

◆

Text: Acts 12:5–16

[5] Peter therefore was kept in prison: but prayer was made without ceasing of the church unto God for him. [6] And when Herod would have brought him forth, the same night Peter was sleeping between two soldiers, bound with two chains: and the keepers before the door kept the prison. [7] And, behold, the angel of the Lord came upon him, and a light shined in the prison: and he smote Peter on the side, and raised him up, saying, Arise up quickly. And his chains fell off from his hands. [8] And the angel said unto him, Gird thyself, and bind on thy sandals. And so he did. And he saith unto him, Cast thy garment about thee, and follow me. [9] And he went out, and followed him; and wist not that it was true which was done by the angel; but thought he saw a vision. [10] When they were past the first and the second ward, they came unto the iron gate that leadeth unto the city; which opened to them of his own accord: and they went out, and passed on through one street; and forthwith the angel departed from him. [11] And when Peter was come to himself, he said, Now I know of a surety, that the Lord hath sent his angel, and hath delivered me out of the hand of Herod, and from all the expectation of the people of the Jews. [12] And when he had considered the thing, he came to the house of Mary the mother of John, whose surname was Mark; where many were gathered together praying. [13] And as Peter knocked at the door of the gate, a damsel came to hearken, named Rhoda. [14] And when she knew Peter's voice, she opened not the gate for gladness, but ran in, and told how Peter stood before the gate. [15] And they said unto her, Thou art mad. But she constantly affirmed that it was even so. Then said they, It is his

angel. [16] But Peter continued knocking: and when they had opened the door, and saw him, they were astonished.

Peter's Power Source Part III
Hooray for Rhoda!
Text: Acts 12:5–16

1. Peter in Prison:

    a.   Peace in your present place

    b.   Provision in your present place

    c.   Power in your present place

2. Power of Prayer:

    a.   People of prayer

    b.   Place of prayer

    c.   Problem with prayer

3. Praise for a Believing Person: (Rhoda)

    a.   Saved sister

    b.   Serving sister

    c.   Shouting sister

Conclusion: Wonder Women

We should be getting to know Peter quite well at this point in our series. The main thing that I want us to learn is that God uses ordinary people. God places the *extra* in us to make us extraordinary. However, we all are ordinary people whom God invites into an extraordinary relationship. When we grasp the fact that God birthed us to bless us, then we are on our way. In spite of your birthplace, birth order, or birth circumstances, God birthed you to bless you. Can you receive that?

Many people never get beyond their circumstances. Give God your today, and your yesterday will not hinder your tomorrow. Acts 12 begins by telling us that King Herod was responsible for killing James, the son of Zebedee. James was as faithful as Peter: one apostle dies for his faith. God's will determines whether we are set free on earth or in heaven. The important thing is that we are obedient.

Peter in Prison:

At this time, the church has several thousand members, but it is only a few months old. It is still in spiritual diapers. It is a baby church. The initial glory days have given way to intense persecution. King Herod has picked out a few of the leaders to pick on them. The Bible says that he wanted to vex them. He had James' head cut off; he knew that this tactic would put fear in the other believers. When he saw that the Jews were pleased with the killing of James, he went for Peter. Whenever your brother or sister is going through spiritual warfare, you should pray for them because, eventually, the devil will come after you. He placed Peter in prison but had to wait until the religious holiday was over before he could kill him. They locked him up with soldiers guarding him in three four-hour shifts.

Peter had peace in prison. How could this preacher sleep so sound in prison? Why is he not stressing?

1. He could sleep because of the promise that God made him. "I will be with you always."

> Verily, verily, I say unto thee, when thou wast young, thou girdedst thyself, and walkedst whither thou wouldest: but when thou shalt be old, thou shalt stretch forth thy hands, and another shall gird thee, and carry thee whither thou wouldest not. (John 21:18)

2. The Lord told him that he would live to be an old man. He is not old, so he is immortal until God is finished with him.

3. Peter has been in prison before. If God paid his bail one time, he will do it again. When you have to go through the same thing a second time, God expects you to be confident and not complain.

Whatever God tells you during the day still holds true at night.

The good news of this text is that you can have peace in your present place. Many of us stress because we have put a timetable on our deliverance and a cap on our praise. If you do not learn to shout before the battle, during the battle, and after the battle, your praise is limited. The power of God has no limits. He can move anytime, any place, and for anybody. If we truly believe Romans 8:28:

> And we know that all things work together for good to them that love God, to them who are the called according to his purpose.

We can say thank you Jesus in every situation. The Word of God is true all of the time or none of the time. Peter is in prison and is on schedule for execution the next day, and he falls sound asleep.

Power of Prayer:

When news of Peter's arrest reached the church, they entered into prayer. Prayer was fervent, earnest, and nonstop.

> For where two or three are gathered together in my name, there am I in the midst of them. (Matthew 18:20)

I have one request that I pray every day: that Pilgrim Baptist Church will become a praying church. I am asking God that we have between sixty and ninety people praying on Tuesdays and Wednesdays. The disciples knew the power of prayer because of their experience in the Upper Room. The prayers of the righteous have great results. You cannot say that you believe in the power of prayer and never pray. God is calling us to be a praying church.

Much prayer, much power; some prayer, some power; no prayer, no power. The churches' prayer summoned God; God summoned an angel; and the angel summoned Peter.

Note the detail of Peter's deliverance:

1. The angel came to the cell.

2. A light shines on Peter.

3. The angel hits him on his side.

4. The chain falls off.

5. "Peter, put on your clothes."

6. "Peter, put on your shoes."

7. "Peter, put your coat on."

8. "Peter, follow me." (Acts 12:5-10)

He is in a dream state, but he follows, past the first set of guards, past the second set of guards, and then the iron gate opens automatically. When Peter walked through the gate, the angel left him. I believe in the present-day ministry of angels.

> Take heed that ye despise not one of these little ones; for I say unto you, that in heaven their angels do always behold the face of my Father, which is in heaven. (Matthew 18:10)
>
> For he shall give his angels charge over thee, to keep thee in all thy ways. (Psalm 91:11)
>
> The angel of the Lord encampeth round about them that fear him, and delivereth them. The one thing we can be sure of is that God still sends angels to help us, but we are to have faith in him and them. (Psalm 34:7)

Peter is free, and he goes directly to the place where they were praying. If you believe in prayer, then make your way to the place of prayer (the apostles didn't say, "I can pray at home." They did not say how busy they were; they just prayed).

Praise for a Believing Person

Peter is free, so he knocks on the door. A young woman comes to the door whose name is Rhoda; her name means rose. She hears Peter's voice, recognizes it, and runs back to the meeting filled with joy.

Rhoda is a child of God. She is sensitive to the Holy Spirit. She heard the knock. She had faith. She could have gone to the door, and an enemy could have been standing there. Faith knows no fear! Rhoda is also a doorkeeper. She is working as a housekeeper, but she does not allow her status to keep her from spiritual things. She shouts loudly that Peter is at the door.

Status and position do not make you spiritual or unspiritual. You can be rich or poor and shout. Shouting comes from experience, not economics. "Rhoda, you are insane. Peter is in jail; that is why we called this prayer meeting," some one present may have said to her. An angel can get Peter out of jail but cannot get him into a prayer meeting. It is so easy to involve yourself in religious activities and not truly believe in what you are doing. Rhoda is crazy for expecting an answer to her prayers.

Have you ever asked God for something and were shocked that he sent the answer? Mothers, wives, sisters, daughters, God has always used you to make a difference. You are more precious than gold when you are saved, serving, and shouting. Rhoda teaches us that one person can make a difference. Do you believe that? Prayer summoned God; God summoned the angel; the angel summoned Peter, but without Rhoda, Peter is still in danger.

Thank God for the prayer meeting. Thank God for the angel. Thank God for Peter, but hooray for Rhoda!

Mothers, wives, sisters, daughters, we praise you. We celebrate you. We rise up and call you blessed. Rhoda means rose. Sometimes a rose has to deal with thorns, but that is all right. One can make a difference.

- Without one Eve, there would be no human race.

- Without one Jochebed, there would be no Moses.

- Without one Deborah, the nation was in chaos.

- Without one Esther, the Jews would have been destroyed.

- Without one Hannah, there would be no Samuel.

- Without one Elizabeth, there would be no John the Baptist.

- Without one Eunice, there would be no Timothy.

- Without one Mary, there would be no Jesus.

Without one Jesus, no salvation, no heaven, no love, no church, no mercy, no grace, no peace, no Bible.

Discussion Questions

1. Discuss Rhoda's part in the story.

2. How do you treat people with a criminal history?

3. Discuss the response of the church to Peter's appearance at the prayer meeting.

4. Have you ever been surprised that God answered a prayer for you?

5. Discuss how God uses women to share good news with others.

6. Discuss how the angel was used by God to release Peter.

7. Discuss the role of women in the church.

Peter's Prejudice

✦

Text: Galatians 2:6–14

[6] But of these who seemed to be somewhat, (whatsoever they were, it maketh no matter to me: God accepteth no man's person:) for they who seemed to be somewhat in conference added nothing to me: [7] But contrariwise, when they saw that the gospel of the uncircumcision was committed unto me, as the gospel of the circumcision was unto Peter; [8] (For he that wrought effectually in Peter to the apostleship of the circumcision, the same was mighty in me toward the Gentiles) [9] And when James, Cephas, and John, who seemed to be pillars, perceived the grace that was given unto me, they gave to me and Barnabas the right hands of fellowship; that we should go unto the heathen, and they unto the circumcision. [10] Only they would that we should remember the poor; the same which I also was forward to do. [11] But when Peter was come to Antioch, I withstood him to the face, because he was to be blamed. [12] For before that certain came from James, he did eat with the Gentiles: but when they were come, he withdrew and separated himself, fearing them which were of the circumcision. [13] And the other Jews dissembled likewise with him; insomuch that Barnabas also was carried away with their dissimulation. [14] But when I saw that they walked not uprightly according to the truth of the gospel, I said unto Peter before them all, If thou, being a Jew, livest after the manner of Gentiles, and not as do the Jews, why compellest thou the Gentiles to live as do the Jews?

Title: Peter's Prejudice
Text: Galatians 2:6–14

1. Peter's Relapse:

    a. His faith

    b. His fear

    c. His fall

2. Paul's Rebuke:

    a. Hypocrisy

    b. Hurtful

    c. Health

3. Peter's Recovery:

    a. Grow in godliness

    b. Grow in goodness

    c. Grow in grace

Conclusion: Good news!

Good habits are easy to make. Bad habits are hard to break. Every person who is serious about dating must develop good dating habits. Anyone starting a career should develop good work habits. Every student that desires success must develop good study habits. Newlyweds must start out right to have a healthy marriage. Parents must raise children right for them to have any chance of being healthy, productive members of the community.

I make this point because in ministry we usually spend most of our energy getting people on track with God. I believe all of us will agree that life is much easier when you are right than it is to get right after living wrong for a long time. I thank God for all of the self-help programs to enable us to deal with the various addictions that we live with; however, I wish we could persuade everyone to live for Christ and God. Remember the saying:

> Sow a thought, reap an act.
>
> Sow an act, reap a behavior.
>
> Sow a behavior, reap a character.
>
> Sow a character, reap a destiny.

As we conclude our study of the life of Peter, we have seen him come a long way. He started by answering the call to follow Jesus. He made a good confession at Caesarea Philippi. He walked on water to get to Jesus. But then he lost his humility, thought he was stronger than he actually was, and denied the Lord. Jesus forgave him and used him mightily on the day of Pentecost. He went on to heal a lame man and raised a young woman from the dead. In the last chapter, we witnessed an angel setting him free from prison, and he showed up at the prayer meeting where they were pleading with God to deliver him.

Peter's Relapse:

Let's enter the meeting. Peter is about to take the microphone at the meeting of RCA: Relapsed Christians Anonymous.

"My name is Peter." Come on, make him feel welcome. Speak to the brother.

"Here is my story. I was doing well as a Christian. I had faith: giving my testimony, preaching, teaching, even healing the sick and raising the dead. God was really using me. I had great faith. I loved to study the Word, pray, and worship God every opportunity that I had. I was walking in the newness of life. I guess you are wondering what happened to me? I hooked back up with the old crowd: James and John, the sons of Zebedee. They were traditional Jewish brothers who wanted the new Gentile believers to be just like them. They believed that you needed Jesus and the law of Moses for salvation. The fact is that I knew better, but I let my old friends influence me with fear."

> [9] On the morrow, as they went on their journey, and drew nigh unto the city, Peter went up upon the housetop to pray about the sixth hour: [10] And he became very hungry, and would have eaten: but while they made ready, he fell into a trance, [11] And saw heaven opened, and a certain vessel descending unto him, as it had been a great sheet knit at the four corners, and let down to the earth: [12] Wherein were all manner of fourfooted beasts of the earth, and wild beasts, and creeping things, and fowls of the air. [13] And there came a voice to him, Rise, Peter; kill, and eat. [14] But Peter said, Not so, Lord; for I have never eaten any thing that is common or unclean. [15] And the voice spake unto him again the second time, What God hath cleansed, that call not thou common. [16] This was done thrice: and the vessel was received up again into heaven. (Acts 10:9–16)

"I told the church how the Holy Spirit fell on the Gentiles after I preached to them just as it did on the Jews. Nevertheless, they pressured me, and I fell. I relapsed."

It takes courage to admit when we are wrong. Many people can never admit when they make a mistake. It ends up on someone else. Most Christians who come to Jesus are sincere in their desire to walk with God. The longer that we are in church, we become more concerned with tradition than the Gospel, and we want people to be more like us than like Jesus. Most Christians relapse or go back to their old ways because they are influenced by someone they thought was spiritual. James and John were more concerned with having Jesus' name than having his nature.

We relapse whenever we take our eyes off God and put them on people or problems.

Paul's Rebuke:

Paul is now on the scene. He has spent years spreading the Gospel to the Gentiles. Just as God had used Peter, he also used Paul. Paul preached that God accepts everyone regardless of his or her color, class, or culture. Back in the day, the strict Jews wanted Gentiles to be second-class Christians if they would not submit to circumcision and keep the law. Paul insisted that God has no favorites. Let me ask these questions, "Do you treat all Christians as brothers and sisters?

Do you welcome all colors, classes, and cultures? Do you value men more highly than women?"

> [26] For ye are all the children of God by faith in Christ Jesus. [27] For as many of you as have been baptized into Christ have put on Christ. [28] There is neither Jew nor Greek, there is neither bond nor free, there is neither male nor female: for ye are all one in Christ Jesus. [29] And if ye be Christ's, then are ye Abraham's seed, and heirs according to the promise. (Galatians 3:26–29)

Here is what happened in Antioch. The Lord sent three men to have Peter come to the Gentile city of Antioch to preach. God moved in a mighty way. The Holy Spirit came with power. Many were saved and Spirit-filled. They invited Peter home after worship. They had barbecue pork ribs, pig's feet, and greens cooked with salt pork. Peter remembered that nothing is unclean, so he grubbed. He ate seconds and took a plate home. They had a good time in the Lord. James and John came to town, and Peter ate with them at the kosher table. He was fearful of what they would say.

Let me take a silent poll. How many of us act one way when we are in one crowd and very different in another crowd? Do you act the same around both saints and sinners? Do you allow certain friends to influence how you interact with people that they do not care for?

Paul states that he confronted Peter to his face. (Acts 15) He said, "Peter, you have relapsed. You are acting funny. You are wishy-washy. You are playing favorites. You are a hypocrite. Barnabas is acting just like you." (paraphrase mine)

When we act differently around different people, we cause those who follow us to act the same way. The church is hurt when we treat people wrongly because they are different. We cannot justify sexism, racism, or classism. How we act affects what others think of Christ and his church.

Dentist's story

A dentist was visiting a church in the East bay and was considering joining the fellowship. At the end of the service, the pastor asked if he might come back. The doctor said that he would not be back. The pastor asked if he would share with him why he would not return. He said the usher who showed him to his seat owed him for a partial bridge; the deacon that prayed owed him for a set of teeth; and the lead soloist who sang, "God is…" owes him for a cleaning.

Peter's Recovery:

Peter changed after Paul confronted him. Proverbs teaches us that a rebuke from a friend is better than a kiss from the wicked. Thank God that Peter belonged to that group of Christians that still loved him when he told the truth.

Peter's story is your story and my story. Peter recovered. He came back. We know that he came back because we have his letters. It is truly a blessing that we can build our dream house of tomorrow out of the ashes we find ourselves in today.

Listen to Peter's second letter:

> [3] According as his divine power hath given unto us all things that pertain unto life and godliness, through the knowledge of him that hath called us to glory and virtue: [4] Whereby are given unto us exceeding great and precious promises: that by these ye might be partakers of the divine nature, having escaped the corruption that is in the world through lust. [5] And beside this, giving all diligence, add to your faith virtue; and to virtue knowledge; [6] And to knowledge temperance; and to temperance patience; and to patience godliness; [7] And to godliness brotherly kindness; and to brotherly kindness charity. [8] For if these things be in you, and abound, they make you that ye shall neither be barren nor unfruitful in the knowledge of our Lord Jesus Christ. [9] But he that lacketh these things is blind, and cannot see afar off, and hath forgotten that he was purged from his old sins. We are to grow in godliness. (2 Peter 1:3–9)

He closes the letter by telling us to grow in grace.

> But grow in grace, and in the knowledge of our Lord and Saviour Jesus Christ. To him be glory both now and for ever. Amen. (2 Peter 3:18)

That is the Word—*grace.* The good news of Jesus Christ is that his grace is sufficient.

Hymn writer:

Robert Robinson, author of the hymn, "Come, Thou Fount of Every Blessing," lost the happy communion with the Savior he had once enjoyed, and in his declining years, he wandered into the byways of sin. As a result, he became deeply troubled in spirit. Hoping to relieve his mind, he decided to travel.

In the course of his journeys, he became acquainted with a young woman who began to talk about spiritual matters. She asked him what he thought of a hymn that she had been reading and to his amazement, it was none other than his own composition. He tried to evade her question, but she continued to press him for a response.

He suddenly began to weep. With tears streaming down his cheeks, he said, "I am the man who wrote that hymn many years ago. I'd give anything to experience again the joy I knew then." Although greatly surprised, she reassured him that the "streams of mercy" mentioned in his song still flowed. Mr. Robinson was deeply touched. Turning his wandering heart to the Lord, he was restored to full fellowship.

This word causes every heart to cheer: *grace.*

Grace…amazing grace.

A promise for every problem, a scripture for every situation, and a commandment for every circumstance.

Grace…It forgives the guilty.

Grace…It removes all shame.

Grace…It heals all hurt.

Grace…It calms every fear.

Grace…It opens the doors of heaven.

Grace…It tells us that God loves us just as we are!

Grace put you to sleep last night and watched over you while you slept and then woke you up.

Grace, I need it, you need it, we all need it, grace!

Discussion Questions

1. What is prejudice?

2. Why is there still so much separation between races, religions, and cultures?

3. Can you identify with Peter?

4. Discuss hypocrisy.

5. Discuss Paul's rebuke of Peter.

6. Why do Christians relapse into old behavior?

7. What can we learn about diversity and inclusion from this story?

Epilogue

Christianity in America is becoming a religion of celebrities. Thirty years ago, you could barely find a celebrity in church. Now ministries are gearing themselves to lure them as an agent would court a first round draft pick! I am not against this trend as much as I am for the Gospel of Jesus Christ. I have preached and taught in ministries ten times larger than my own. I will admit that I love preaching to large audiences. While the media and the ministers tout the buildings, budgets, and baptisms of the mega ministries, I hear the words of Jesus:

> [16] And he came to Nazareth, where he had been brought up: and, as his custom was, he went into the synagogue on the sabbath day, and stood up for to read. [17] And there was delivered unto him the book of the prophet Esaias. And when he had opened the book, he found the place where it was written, [18] The Spirit of the Lord is upon me, because he hath anointed me to preach the gospel to the poor; he hath sent me to heal the brokenhearted, to preach deliverance to the captives, and recovering of sight to the blind, to set at liberty them that are bruised, [19] To preach the acceptable year of the Lord. [20] And he closed the book, and he gave it again to the minister, and sat down. And the eyes of all them that were in the synagogue were fastened on him. (Luke 4:16–20)

I believe that if we cater too much to the up and in, we might lose sight of the down and out. Many of the large ministries do a great job in fulfilling both commissions of social betterment and evangelization of the sinner. I just want to make a case for those like Peter and myself. I was born in poverty and raised in a single-family home. I never met my biological father.

My religious training was nonexistent, since my mother worked on Sundays. Although I was a good student, the call of the world was more than I could resist. I dropped out of high school and landed in a youth facility for almost eight months. It was there that a counselor encouraged me to finish high school and made me believe that I was college material.

I have been blessed to travel to foreign countries to preach, but it is by the grace of God. When I think of the many young men and women who are dead or in prison that were no worse than I was, I have to praise God. My mother was proud of the fact that I never allowed my education or my blessings to lead to pride. I want to cast a vote for the community of mistake makers. Consider the eleventh chapter of Hebrews. It is referred to as the "faith" hall of fame. Read the chapter again, and it will read like a hall of shame, were it not for God's intervention.

Meet Noah the drunk.

Meet Abraham the liar.

Meet Isaac the deceived.

Meet Jacob the deceiver.

Meet Joseph the braggart.

Meet Moses the murderer.

Meet Samson the promiscuous.

Meet David the sinner-king.

The common denominator in each of their lives is God. I know that many in our world need to hear that God can still bring misfits to maturity.

Therefore if any man be in Christ, he is a new creature: old things are passed away; behold, all things are become new. (2 Corinthians 5:17)

Jesus Christ was Peter's hope and he will be ours also.

The maturity that we long for cannot be attained through human effort. Paul learned the hard way that in his flesh dwells nothing good (see Romans 7–8). It is the work of the Holy Spirit to convict us of our immaturity. It is also the Spirit that delivers us from it as well. There are millions who do not believe that they are worthy of God's love. Their past mistakes have left them in a state of paralysis. The question that the Lord asked the prophet Ezekiel is worth repeating, "Can these bones live?"(Ezekiel 37:3) The landscape of mistake makers is strewn with dry bones. Can they live again? It is worth noting that the remedy for the bones was Spirit-filled preaching. When Peter recovered, that is what God assigned him to do! The paradox is that God uses our mistakes more than our successes to win a lost world back to God.

I would never boast of sin. However, my mistakes have led to my maturity. I believe that Peter and many others would add. Amen!

Bibliography

Bruce, F.F. *The Book of Acts*. Grand Rapids, Michigan: William B.Eerdmans Publishing Company, 1988.

Covey, Stephen R. *First Things First*. Simon & Schuster, 1994.New York London Toronto Sydney Tokyo Singapore.

Fernando, Ajith. *The NIV Application Commentary*. Grand Rapids, Michigan: Zondervan Publishing, 1998.

Gaebelein, Frank E., general editor. *The Expositors Bible Commentary*. Grand Rapids, Michigan: Zondervan Publishing, Vols. 8–10,12.

Goodman—Phillips, Karon *You're Late Again Lord*. Uhrichsville, Ohio: Barbour Publishing Inc., 2002.

Hybels, Bill. *Who You are When No One is Looking*. Downers Grove, Illinois: InterVarsity Press, 1987.

Lotz, Anne Graham. *Just Give Me Jesus*. Nashville, Tennessee: W Publishing Group, 2000.

Lucado, Max. *Just like Jesus*. Nashville, Tennessee: Word Publishing, 1998.

Maxwell, John. *Failing Forward*. Nashville, Tennessee: Thomas Nelson Publishing, 2000.

Swindoll, Charles, R. *The Finishing Touch*. Nashville, Tennessee: Word Publishing, 1994.

Wiersbe, Warren. *Be Mature*. Colorado Springs, Colorado: Chariot Victor Publishing, 1978.

978-0-595-36777-1
0-595-36777-1

Printed in the United States
44029LVS00006B/376-1008